NOLS
Bear Essentials

Published by
STACKPOLE BOOKS
5067 Ritter Road
Mechanicsburg, PA 17055
www.stackpolebooks.com

Printed in the United States of America

First edition

10 9 8 7 6 5 4 3 2 1

Cover design by Caroline Stover
Cover photograph courtesy of Thomas D. Mangelsen, www.mangelsen.com

Library of Congress Cataloging-in-Publication Data
Reed, Tom, 1961–
   NOLS Bear Essentials : hiking and camping in bear country /
John Gookin and Tom Reed. John Gookin and Tom Reed. — 1st ed.
      p. cm.
   Includes index.
   ISBN-13: 978-0-8117-3549-0 (alk. paper)
   ISBN-10: 0-8117-3549-4 (alk. paper)
   1. Black bear—Behavior. 2. Grizzly bear—Behavior. 3. Camping—
Safety measures. 4. Hiking—Safety measures. 5. Bear attacks—
North America—Prevention. 6. Outdoor recreation—North
America—Safety measures. I. Gookin, John. II. Title.

QL737.C27R44 2009
796.5028'9—dc22

                                                                    2008051645

NOLS
Bear Essentials

Hiking and Camping in Bear Country

John Gookin
and Tom Reed

STACKPOLE
BOOKS

Contents

Acknowledgments

Sincere thanks to our colleagues in the field of bear management for their help in reviewing the text of this book. Any errors in combining their various expert opinions are ours, not theirs.

Tom Smith, Brigham Young University,
Bear Researcher

Brian Debolt, Wyoming Game & Fish,
Bear Management Officer

Mark Bruscino, Wyoming Game & Fish,
Bear Management Officer

Bill Stiver, Great Smoky Mountains
National Park, Wildlife Biologist

Victoria Serer, Yosemite National Park,
Bear Manager

Ben Tabor, New York Department of
Environmental Conservation,
Wildlife Technician

Introduction

Welcome to bear country! Bears are clever, powerful, and magnificent animals. Like people, each bear is unique, so the advice in this book is general in nature and can't prepare you for every behavior of every bear. Since 1965, NOLS has camped in bear country for over three million nights with only one injury directly caused by a bear, so the practices used by NOLS to camp and hike in bear country are based on significant experience. We also stay in touch with some of the world's top bear scientists and have taken a leadership role in developing techniques that help us coexist with wild bears. But even with this cumulative expertise, we still consider ourselves to be constant students of bear behavior.

Our most important attitude is one best explained by the Koyukon people of Alaska. Anthropologist Richard Nelson's book *Make Prayers to the Raven: A Koyukon View of the Northern Forest* portrays the Koyukon people living harmoniously with bears for thousands of years. We are visiting bears in their home, and if we learn about bears and respect them in their natural habitat, our two species can coexist.

Your decision to camp in bear country comes with responsibilities to camp and hike in ways that respect the natural activities of bears. This isn't as complicated as it might seem. It takes a little knowledge about bears and a lot of self-discipline. Campers who respect the natural habits of bears can usually coexist with bears with few problems. Keep the following points in mind:

A fed bear is a dead bear. Bears that receive food from humans, intentionally or not, develop dangerous unnatural habits and are often destroyed. In some areas, wildlife managers try moving them away from human activity first, but a lot of these bears do eventually get euthanized. Many wildlife managers have given up on attempts to move problem animals, because in their areas it just postpones the inevitable once a bear·has been conditioned by humans to seek us out for food.

A fed bear is a deadly bear. Wild bears have very few interactions with people. They usually avoid us like the plague. But once people start feeding bears, these bears become food-conditioned and habituated to people. Wild bears that become more comfortable around people are extremely dangerous. Studies have shown that many bear-caused human injuries are associated with habituated, food-conditioned bears (Herrero, 2002). The people who get hurt by these bears are often not the folks who give the bears the most food initially, but the future campers who are approached by these habituated bears.

Bears have an incredible sense of smell. One summer a whale washed ashore from the Beaufort Sea and shortly thereafter satellite-tracked polar bears started swimming towards it from up to 120 km (75 miles) away. Sense of smell is much more significant for bears than for people. Once bears get a small food reward and associate that food's smell with the smell of humans, they easily detect your food (and you) from miles away. They also are curious about smells and might come exploring if they smell something new.

Problem bears aren't born that way; they are trained by people. Campers who have sloppy camps or somehow give bears positive rewards for coming near humans cause most backcountry bear problems. A lack of negative consequences associated with coming near people leads to habituation. The bears learn to associate food with the smell of humans, and the rewards condition the bears to become more comfortable around people. This is elementary bear psychology.

Bears fear other bears. Bear ecologists say that when bears have nightmares they don't dream of humans, they dream of other bears. Thirteen to forty-four percent of young grizzly bears get killed by an adult bear, depending on the region (Schwartz, Miller & Haroldson, 2003, p. 590). Since bears usually have twins, many surviving bears have seen a brother or sister get killed by another bear. This has some important effects on bear behavior:

- sows are extremely protective of their cubs, and
- bears that are surprised by humans often react to defend themselves.

Most bears avoid encounters with other aggressive animals. Bears often view people simply as they would another bear: some are threats, and some are not.

A bear is not just a bear. In low-density areas (with fewer bears per square kilometer), bears are used to more personal space. In high-density areas, bears are used to less personal space. We refer to how close another bear, or a person, needs to get to a bear before it displays an obvious response to intrusion into its personal space as its overt response distance. For comparison, in Katmai National Park, where you might see 40 to 60 bears per day, bears only require 50 to 100 meters of personal space. But in interior Alaska, where there is a much lower density of bears, they might need a kilometer or more of personal space. Always check in with the local land managers about how to deal effectively with the bears in their specific areas, and as a general rule, keep your distance.

We hope this small book of bear essentials will help you learn about bears so you will understand them well enough to coexist with them peacefully. If you continue to camp in bear country, pick up more books about bears to learn as much as you can about them and about what has gone wrong with bear-human interactions in the past. We hope you enjoy being a lifelong learner about bear camping as much as we do.

Bear Habitat
& IDENTIFICATION

HABITAT
Bears are symbolic of wild country, synonymous with the great outdoors. Human cultures evolved side-by-side with bears, and today, though their habitat is shrinking sharply and their numbers are on the decline in many places, bears still occupy much of North America. NOLS has no expertise with bears outside of North America, so populations of bears in other parts of the world are not covered by this book.

Two main species of bears roam the forests and mountains of our continent—the black bear (*Ursus americanus*) and the brown bear (*Ursus arctos*). Of the two, the black bear is the more common, consisting of two basic subspecies, the American black bear and the Asiatic black bear. The brown bear is larger, more aggressive, less common, and is often identified interchangeably with its subspecies *Ursus arctos horribilis*, the grizzly bear. Polar bears (*Ursus maritimus*), which are imperiled by global climate changes and occupy a thin layer of Arctic habitat rarely frequented by humans, are not covered in this book.

As a reminder of the exact definitions used for taxonomy, a *species* is a genetic group that can interbreed. A *population* is a local group that interbreeds: it can still breed with other populations of the same species if it has the opportunity. A *subspecies* is a population that is geographically isolated and has distinctive characteristics. It is designated with a third specific name such as *horribilis* for the grizzly subspecies of brown bears.

The American black bear lives in forty-one of the fifty United States, all of the Canadian provinces, and south into Mexico. It is widely hunted and its numbers are steady, if not increasing.

Brown bears are found across the north-western edge of North America, from Alaska to northcentral Canada, and down into the Rockies. In Alaska, *brown bear* is used by scientists for the coastal subspecies and *grizzly* for interior bears. Furthermore, Kodiak bears (*Ursus arctos middendorffi*) have their own distinctive features and are the largest of the brown bears. Even in the Lower 48, *brown* and *grizzly* are sometimes used locally to refer to two different populations, but this is sometimes just local jargon. There are no significant behavior differences between brown and grizzly bears, so this book will use the names grizzly and brown interchangeably.

In general, black bears are creatures of the woods—from eastern hardwoods to Sierra conifers and from Alaskan spruce woods to Mexican pine forests. They are omnivores and opportunists, eating everything from grubs, roots, and berries to beefsteak stolen from a summer barbecue. Generally a shy animal, they, like their more aggressive grizzly cousins, are also extremely intelligent. A black bear never forgets where it got its last meal, and it remembers behaviors and techniques that worked to snag that dinner. There are tales and photographs of black bears dangling from wires to pull down bird feeders, black bears climbing monkey-like up trees and telephone poles, and bears in cabin kitchens and horse barn grain bins.

The grizzly bear evolved a bit differently and remains in somewhat different habitat than the black bear. In general, the grizzly is more comfortable in open country, whether the historic high plains of North America's bison steppes or the big tundra of Alaska. Grizzly bears are found in only a few remnant populations in the Lower 48, primarily around Glacier and Yellowstone National Parks. In those places, the grizzly has proven to be adaptable enough to live year-round in thick forests, particularly near Glacier.

Coastal brown bears are more dependent upon spawning runs of salmon, lush coastal vegetation, and sometimes marine animals for survival. In most cases it is more carnivorous than its interior relative and—as a result of all of the fish protein—much larger. In general, scientists see the grizzly and brown bears as one species: the brown bear a resident of coast-lines and the grizzly an interior bear.

All bears are omnivores, meaning they'll eat just about anything—from roots and berries, to human refuse, to insect larvae, to ungulates, to fish. This means they can be found in many habitats. Grizzly bears, for example, once lived in prairie coulees and ate bison meat. Today, they range all the way to the Arctic Circle, fol-lowing ripening berry crops and taking the occasional caribou calf. Black bears have spent lifetimes within the city limits of western mountain towns and have been known to pester campers on the Appalachian Trail.

In some places, the ranges of grizzly and black bears overlap and it is possible to see both black and grizzly bears on the same day, and in some instances, in the same location, such as feeding sites like fish spawning runs. Expect the black bears in these areas to distance themselves from the grizzlies in either space or time: that is, the black bears either feed away from the grizzlies, or they become more nocturnal to avoid the grizzlies.

IDENTIFICATION

If you are hiking in the deep woods and you see a small dark bear, is it always going to be a black bear? Or if you are hiking above timberline and see a huge light-colored bear turning over rocks as it looks for insects, is it always going to be a grizzly bear?

The answer to both questions is no. With bears, there are few hard and fast rules except two: color and size alone are not reliable indicators of bear species. Grizzly bears can have a dark, almost black coat, and immature grizzlies are often quite small. Black bears can be found in many color phases, including a blonde color that looks very much like the coat of many grizzlies. They also can get quite large.

In general, though, black bears are smaller than grizzlies. The average adult black bear in the Intermountain West weighs between 100 and 300 pounds. Grizzly bears in the same region can range from 200 to 350 pounds for females and 300 to 650 pounds for males. Alaska's coastal grizzlies (brown bears), supping on salmon and sedges in the Land of the Midnight Sun, are the big daddies of the bruin family, sometimes tipping the scales at over 1,000 pounds.

Since size and coat color are not reliable identifiers, what are? It takes a combination of reliable characteristics to properly distinguish between black and grizzly bears. Most bear experts agree that telling the difference between grizzlies and black bears comes down to several factors: the evidence of powerful shoulders or a shoulder hump, the facial profile, the ear shape, the claws, and the tracks. Obviously, if you only get a glimpse of a bear, it is very difficult to tell what species it is, especially if the bear is coming at you and your

BLACK BEAR

GRIZZLY BEAR

judgment, vision, and bladder are all causing
you trouble.

Grizzlies are diggers. They love to turn
over rocks and can spend hours digging up a
hillside in an attempt to snack on one ground
squirrel. Consequently, they have a massive
hump of muscle and bone on their shoulders—
a hump that can be seen in profile, and even
when the bear is facing the observer. Black
bears do not have this hump on their shoulders; rather, their profile is straight or sloped
downward from rump to head. The grizzly is
like a powerful body-builder, shaped like an

anvil with huge shoulders. The black bear is like a pear-shaped couch jockey, with sloping shoulders and a large behind.

The facial profile is a good indicator of species type. Grizzlies have a well-defined dish shape to their heads; in other words, the nose from the edge of the brow dips down. Black bears have a much straighter profile, with the nose coming straight off the brow in a clean line, giving them a long, pointy-nose with a slight hump on it, often referred to as a Roman nose.

Ear shape, too, is a good indicator of bear type. Mature grizzlies have smaller, more rounded ears set far apart on their heads. Ears on black bears are pointed, appear to be larger, and are set closer together on the head.

Claw shape is another way to tell one bear species from another. Of course, if you are close enough to a live bear to observe the character of its claws, you are too darned close. We are usually looking at tracks when assessing claws. Grizzly claws are adapted for digging and are relatively straight and gently curved. They can be larger than a human adult's finger. Black bear claws are curved significantly and usually not much larger than two inches long.

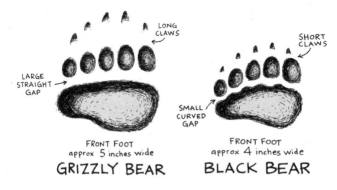

LONG CLAWS

SHORT CLAWS

LARGE STRAIGHT GAP

SMALL CURVED GAP

FRONT FOOT
approx 5 inches wide

GRIZZLY BEAR

FRONT FOOT
approx 4 inches wide

BLACK BEAR

Grizzly claws are dull on the tips, whereas black bear claws are very sharp, enabling them to climb limbless trees.

What if you don't actually see a bear, but you find a good track near your camp in the mud? There are several ways to tell a grizzly track from a black bear track.

In general, a grizzly front track is squarer in shape than a black bear track. Place a straight-edged item like a pencil between the edge of the paw pad parallel to and between the toes. If the ends of the pencil intersect with the toes on either side of the track, it is probably a black bear track. If the pencil does not inter-sect—in other words, if the toe pads run in a nearly straight line off the front of the foot—it is probably a grizzly or brown bear track. If you can see imprints of claw marks greater than two inches in front of the toe pads, that also indicates a grizzly track.

Identifying bears correctly is important. People who enter bear habitat with both black and grizzly bears need to learn how to differentiate between the two species. It can help you make a good decision should you encounter a bear. However, regardless of what kind of a bear you see, remember that if you are in the backcountry, you are in its living room. You are a guest in its house, so act accordingly.

Bear
BEHAVIOR

Every bear is as individual and unique as every human is. The primary generalities we use in this book are that 1) most bears naturally avoid humans, so our careful behavior helps them stay away from us, and 2) once in a blue moon we'll meet a predatory bear, roughly as rare as a human serial killer, so we want to be ready to defend ourselves against that rare predatory bear.

We mentioned earlier that black bears evolved in forested environments; thus, they have adopted a cryptic behavior strategy, one that is consistent with that environment: Why fight when you can safely flee? That is precisely what nearly 100 percent of them do when presented with conflict. The response evolved in encounters with other bears, grizzlies in particular, but also even larger, more dominant black bears.

Grizzly bears, on the other hand, evolved on open, treeless tundra where fleeing was not always an option, so their defense strategy includes a good offense. They put up an explosive display of strength and readiness to fight, a bear vs. bear strategy that stands down other ursine aggressors. The problem humans have is that we cannot take the paw swats and nips that bears give other bears—so we suffer terribly.

Beyond these generalities of species, though, there are other factors to consider when trying to understand bear behavior as it regards food or human encounters—genetics, seasons of the year, food availability, bear population densities, locations, previous outcomes in human interactions, and, finally, how you behave when you see a bear. That last item is perhaps the most important factor in bear behavior: the human, not the bear.

How you act and react in bear country often impacts how a bear will act and react. Keeping items that can attract a bear at your rural home or when camping in bear country has as great an influence on bear behavior as anything. A home or camp where food is left readily available to bears will increase your chances of having a bear encounter. Dog food, human food, bird feed, livestock feed, trash cans, and other refuse are all attractants that can reel in a hungry bear. In addition, more and more humans in the United States are building homes in bear country, particularly on property adjacent to public land, and more of us are visiting and recreating in bear country; Yellowstone National Park alone sees three million visitors a year. With humans on the rise in bear country—whether they build a home and stay, or pitch a tent and eventually leave—the odds of encounters with bears are increasing.

How you respond when you encounter a bear is always a determining factor in a bear's behavior—and a whole chapter in this book is dedicated to this topic. First know that both black bears and grizzly bears are highly intelligent. They remember from year to year where they get food. If you camp in a place where a camper from a year before left a filthy camp and gave a bear a free meal, you may unintentionally be setting yourself up for an encounter with that same bear a year later. No matter how clean you keep yourself and your camp, you may pay for another's carelessness without even knowing it. The bear doesn't much care if you are an innocent and thoughtful camper; it just remembers where it got his last meal, and it remembers where it got a meal last year or even five years ago.

There are people who are so afraid of encounters with bears that they only camp in places where there are no bears, just as there are people who avoid swimming in the ocean because of sharks. But to other people, bear country adds something—a sense of adventure to a wild experience that is a remnant of another time when humans weren't the toughest critters to walk the forest. These folks enjoy bear country, they do their homework, and they travel right, with an eye to the ethical way of behaving and with a quality called respect in their hip pockets.

Bear Awareness
& AVOIDANCE

Being alert counts. It matters whether you are crossing the street in the most populous city in the world or shrugging into a backpack and heading out into the wildest country on the planet. Common sense—like knowing not to step into traffic against the light—plays a crucial role in how well and how long we live our lives. In bear country, this means two things: doing your homework and keeping your eyes open. Awareness and avoidance.

DO YOUR HOMEWORK
Talk to local wildlife and land managers before you go into the backcountry. Send them an email asking about the bear country you'll be visiting. Call them up and ask questions. It's part of their job to help you. Have there been any encounters between bears and humans recently in the area where you're going? Are

there any special regulations? What kinds of bears live in the area? What are the common problems there?

BE BEAR AWARE

As you travel in bear country, you'll begin to learn more about a bear's habitat and habits. At first, talking to the land manager will help you. So too will going with a friend who is a seasoned veteran of bear country. You'll begin to pick up techniques and recognize signs that bears are in the area.

You can ask yourself a series of questions, too, particularly in grizzly country. In places where only black bears live, the most likely place to encounter them is where there is food, like in your camp. Conversely, in grizzly country, you may not only camp differently, but you will travel with a new respect. If you notice fresh signs or prime habitat either avoid the area or stay hyper-alert. Here are some questions to ask yourself:

Terrain

How far can I see? Can a bear see me? Could I surprise a bear at close range here? Is the sound of a river drowning out our noise?

Would a bear feel cornered or surprised in this terrain? Does the bear have an escape route that is not right over the top of me?

Weather
Which way is the wind blowing? Will a bear smell us? Is precipitation affecting visibility or the group's attention level? Could a hot day mean that bears are shaded up for the afternoon? Could a cool day mean that they are more active?

Signs and Seasons
Are there any signs of bears in the area, such as tracks, scat, hair, day beds, digs, browsed or broken shrubs, or claw markings on logs or trees? If so, how fresh are they? Are there signs of cubs? How old are they? (Cubs are usually born in February.) Are there any strange odors such as rotting meat or the musky smell of a nearby bear? Is it mating season (May to July)? Are the bears bulking up for winter (August to October)?

Food
Is there an abundance of white bark pine nuts (one type of bear food) around? Are elk calving

or trout spawning in the area? Are there signs of ants, moist plants, berries, roots, or moths? Do you see overturned rocks or torn-apart logs?

The Human Factor
Are you in a high human-use area that might indicate bear habituation to people? Is it hunting season? How experienced is your group? Do they care about doing the right thing in bear country?

AVOID BEARS ON THE TRAIL
Make noise to avoid surprising a grizzly bear. Clap, sing, and talk. This is especially important if visibility is less than 150 yards. In thick timber or dense willows, bears often bed down during the day and can be surprised easily.

Hike in groups. Many bear attacks happen to solo hunters or hikers; small groups of two to three people rarely get attacked; and groups of four or more almost never get attacked. If you can avoid being alone, you are better prepared to avoid a bear encounter and attack.

The lead person in each hiking group should be packing bear spray, ready for quick use, though, ideally, everyone in your hiking group should have bear spray readily available. Bear spray packed deep inside a back-pack or daypack is as useless as not having bear spray at all. Bear sprays come with holsters that can be tied to a belt or an outside pack loop for a quick draw. At night the spray should be either in the tent vestibule or actually in your tent. Used properly, bear spray works, but it does have limitations. Bear spray isn't mosquito repellant; you'll go through a lot of pain and stinging, watering eyes if you spray it on yourself. Do not stay in an area that has been sprayed, and do not spray yourself, your equipment, or around your camp. If any residue is left on clothes, tents, or equipment, rinse them thoroughly with water. Besides being an irritant to humans, lingering odors of bear spray seem to attract some bears.

Look for fresh bear signs. Scat, tracks, clawed trees, dug-up roots, torn-up logs, food caches (partially buried carcasses or places smelling of decayed flesh), or overturned rocks all indicate the presence of a bear. Remain alert, take a wide detour, and make more noise because the bear may be nearby, sleeping off his last meal.

Give a wide berth to feeding areas. Salmon or trout spawning areas, berry patches, lush

While hiking, keep your eyes open for signs of bears in the area—tracks, clawed trees, and torn-up logs.

meadows in the spring and summer, alpine zones with talus slopes in early fall, and white bark pine stands in late fall are popular feeding areas for bears.

Be observant when hiking at dawn or dusk when bears are more active.

If you need to "visit Mother Nature" (go to the bathroom) while hiking, find a spot fairly close to your group, be alert, make lots of noise, and carry your bear spray.

Bears can move very quickly. Based on a sprinting speed of 35 mph, an angry male grizzly can cover 100 yards in about six seconds, which is faster than you just read this sentence. That means he is going from 0 to 35 mph in five jumps! A sow with cubs can reach you from 300 yards away in 20 seconds, which is faster than you just read this paragraph.

AVOID BEARS IN CAMP

In remote camps, sleeping areas must be at least 100 meters uphill, up valley, and upwind of the camp kitchen to prevent evening, down-valley breezes from carrying food odors through the tent sites. Remember, bears have a tremendous sense of smell and will follow odors from downwind.

Bears have night vision that appears to be about as good as ours is, or just a little bit better, so they usually stick to game trails at night, especially on dark moonless nights. Camp sufficiently far from trails to reduce the chances of bear problems at night.

Leave snacks, garbage, used bear spray, and all odorous toiletries like toothpaste, sunscreen, and mosquito repellent properly stored in the kitchen. Do not take any food or fragrant items into your sleeping area.

Avoid sleeping alone outside your tent or fly.

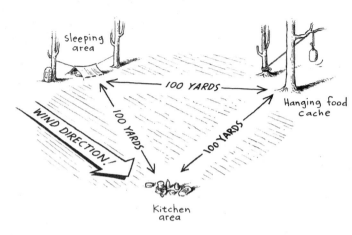

It is always a good idea to have your bear spray handy. This means packing it around on your belt during the day, wearing it just as you would a belt knife. You'll get in the habit of having it on you. At night, bring it into your tent and keep it within reach just like you do with a flashlight.

When visiting the bathroom, stay close to camp. Bring bear spray and make noise.

Studies show that menstruation does not attract bears or provoke attacks. However, used tampons are odorous and should be stored with other possible attractants.

If you can, find a kitchen area far away from your sleeping area on a gravel bar of a large stream or river (when this is permissible). This concentrates the impact on the gravel bar and keeps food smells out of the sleeping area. Your site should have good visibility—at least 150 meters—in all directions. If you can't cook on a gravel bar or by a large river, group the kitchens in an open meadow or clearing. Be sure to abide by local regulations: in some areas your kitchen may be required to be 200 feet from a water source, which is why NOLS doesn't use this practice in Wyoming but does use it frequently in Alaska.

Locate multiple kitchen sites close together so people can gather quickly if a bear is sighted.

Avoid food spills and don't wipe your hands on clothing.

Wash your hands and face after eating. After you are done, leave the food in the food storage area.

Eat food immediately after preparation. Cook only what you can eat and eat everything. Food is tough to burn up thoroughly in a campfire, and the stuff you don't eat you have to pack out of the mountains and carry around as trash. Trash begins to stink, and a bear follows his nose and is a slave to his stomach.

Minimize the use of soap and use local guidelines for disposal of dishwater. Collect all visible food debris from your dishwater and put it into your trash. Scatter dishwater over the soil, or as some land managers may recommend, dump rinse water into a large river or the ocean if you haven't used soap. (A single drop of soap easily contaminates 1,000 gallons of clear water, and "biodegradable" soap just means that within 6 months it will become 90 percent decayed by bacteria, so its short-term water pollution effect is just as problematic.) Soapless dishwater with a few tiny food particles is no more harmful to a stream than are pine needles and leaves unless your particles are large enough to be visible and cause an aesthetic impact.

Food
STORAGE

CAR CAMPING AND FRONT-COUNTRY FOOD STORAGE
Frontcountry campsites, within an easy walk of your car, generally offer more consistent food rewards for bears than backcountry sites do, so those sites have more food conditioned and habituated bears. We can only speculate as to why this is: maybe people camping in the frontcountry don't know or care how to practice the bare essentials of bear camping, or maybe they don't realize that the potential of a bear encounter in the frontcountry is still a possibility.

Check for local instructions about how to camp in frontcountry campgrounds. If there are food storage boxes, use them. You can store food in your car in some areas, but be careful in high use areas like Yosemite Valley, where bears have learned to break into cars; if a bear smells food, it may break a window or even rip your

A classic example of a bear in Yosemite Valley wreaking havoc on a vehicle while trying to get to food. PHOTO COURTESY OF YOSEMITE NATIONAL PARK

car door open to steal your food. These smash-and-grabs probably started with bears crawling through open car windows. Once again, the people who left their food available to bears gave them positive rewards that conditioned them to come to the area for food. When these behaviors go on for long enough that sows teach their cubs these tricks, it is almost impossible to get the bears to leave humans alone without destroying the bears. This is why it is illegal in some parks to store food in your car.

Pet chow is bear chow. Pet food must be stored properly. Feed your pet at a regular feeding time, and then put the leftovers away. Clean up any spillage. Don't let your pet run free, because a curious dog that finds a bear will probably get chased by that bear, and the pet often runs and hides behind its master. Good luck with this scenario.

All trash needs to go in a bear-proof trash can or dumpster. If you need to pour liquid kitchen waste into the ground in the backcountry, do so away from your camp and use a strainer to catch food particles that should be disposed of properly.

Remember: if you give the bears any food reward, they'll be back for more, and they will generally be more aggressive about it the next time.

BACKCOUNTRY FOOD STORAGE

Careful storage of food is critical for the safety of both humans and bears. Many bear scientists believe that wild bears are more afraid of the smell of humans than they are attracted by the smell of humans' food. But not all bears are that wild because careless campers have given them positive rewards that have conditioned them to take more risks around people for the sake of getting food. Preventing and avoiding these food-conditioned bears are the reason we modify our camping habits in bear country. Again, the first thing you need to do is to learn about the local bears from the local wildlife or land managers. Their advice supersedes any of the general advice here because they know *their* bears. For instance, Yosemite bears will keep you up all night long if you just hang your food; bear canisters are the best option there, and they are often the *only* legal option in the Sierra Nevada. In Yellowstone National Park, however, your only legal backcountry option is to hang your food. There may also be local regulations you need to abide by. These regulations might differ between your local national park and the adjoining national forest, and they might differ again from the adjoining state park.

Here is what we typically teach and do at NOLS (when local regulations allow us to!):

Where you cook and store your food is critical in keeping the food's odors from drawing a problem bear into your camp while you are sleeping. On calm nights, cool, heavy air flows down valleys, carrying odors with it. Bears follow those odors back upwind. This means you will gain a strategic advantage by placing your kitchen and food storage site more downwind of your camp, so a bear won't need to go through your camp to get to your food. We usually keep this food site at least 100 meters from our camp. When there are other groups nearby, you don't want someone else's food just upwind of your tent either, sending a plume of odors right over you.

At night, bears feel and smell their way along trails, like a human stumbling along in the dark. Deny access to bears on dark nights by keeping your food storage site away from trails.

How you cook matters. In prime bear habitat, it takes more time to be careful. Bear camping takes time and attention to detail. Schedules should allow adequate time for kitchen setup, cooking, and food storage before dark. Don't spill anything. Frying bacon may invite problems because of splattering grease, so if bears are a huge concern, leave the bacon at home. Impeccable kitchen habits are as important for protecting the bear from habituation to human foods as they are for our own safety.

Store any bear attractants, such as spices, garbage, toothpaste, and fragrant toiletries with your food. This list includes anything that can give a bear a positive food reward or even just attract a bear. If bear signs are abundant, consider also hanging cooking gear, dishes, eating utensils, cleaning knives, fishing equipment, and maybe even any outer clothes worn while cooking. Sometimes campers even wear an apron while cooking that is later stored with the other attractants.

Store food properly at night or any other time it will be unattended. NOLS courses have seen problem bears hit their food stores while people were still in the area. If you are in an area known for problem bears, you need to be as fastidious as asking someone to watch the stove while you go fetch water.

How you store food depends on many factors including local regulations, resources available to you, how long your expedition is, and how big your group is. None of the systems noted above are bear-*proof*, but they are all bear-*resistant*, which means they typically offer enough of a deterrent that the bear gives up trying to get the food long before it gets a food reward. A determined bear, well-trained by sloppy campers, can get almost any food stored outside of a bank vault.

Bear-resistant canisters

Although bulky and heavy, these plastic containers (see illustration) are convenient and allow you to store your food securely when there are no trees from which to hang it. A typical bear canister weighs about three pounds, holds about six days of dry dense food, and costs approximately $70. Using a canister is a great plan for a weekend trip for two people, if it is legal. (You would be required to hang the canister in Yellowstone National Park, so why bother with it?) Some canisters are watertight; others actually trap rainwater. Some bear canisters can be used as a small stool to sit on. In general, the canister system works fine on small, short trips, but not for large groups or long expeditions.

Bear-resistant panniers

Horse packers (people who camp with packhorses carrying their gear) have the option of using panniers (like bike panniers) that are bear-resistant. These aluminum or plastic "backpacks" for horses cost $200 to $400 each, and each hold about as much as a medium-sized cooler. Many outfitters in grizzly country swear by them.

Hanging Food

Most regulations (where applicable) say food must be hung ten feet above the ground (as high as a basketball hoop) and four feet away from both tree trunks and overhanging limbs or poles. Some grizzlies, like the long-legged Kodiak bears, have a reach greater than ten feet, so consider hanging the food twelve feet from the ground and five feet from trees for maximum protection when the locals advise it. Some talented black bears will get your food by messing with your ropes. There are numerous ways to hang your food. Some require climbing one or more trees; some do not. On longer expeditions (10 days or more), consider using a combination of a canister and a small food hang for the first few days.

Single-Rope Hang

A single rope thrown over a stout limb works fine for a lightweight food bag or two. Just find

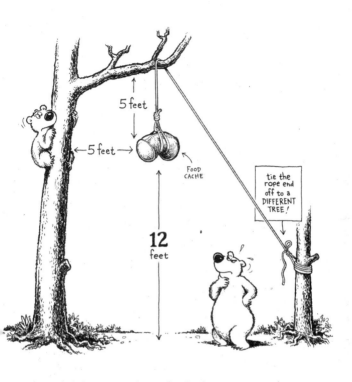

5 feet

← 5 feet →

FOOD CACHE

tie the rope end off to a DIFFERENT TREE!

12 feet

a solid, horizontal tree limb about twenty feet above the ground with no branches below. Throw the rope over the limb. You can weight the end of the rope with a carabiner or a stuff sack with some small rocks in it to make the toss more effective. Some people throw parachute cord as a messenger line and then haul up the bear rope. Once the rope is over the limb, tie the food bags on, haul them up, and tie off the rope to a nearby tree.

There are some disadvantages to this system. Friction from the rope running over the branch makes it hard to haul up heavy food bags. Some people use a long stick to help push the food bags higher while someone else pulls on the rope. The tree limb can be damaged or broken by the rope. Avoid standing under the limb when others are pulling the rope or you risk the famous roadrunner-coyote pile driver scenario.

Double-Rope

This technique reduces friction around trees. Throw one rope over a limb, find an end, tie a figure-eight on a bight, and attach a carabiner (or a pulley). Clip the midpoint of your second rope into the carabiner. Haul the rope up until the carabiner is just below the limb, and tie it off by wrapping it around a nearby tree. Now raise your foodbags using the second rope that is hooked through the carabiner and tie it off. A light pulley makes it much easier to haul the bags up.

Two Tree Hang

If you are unable to find stout horizontal limbs, find two trees near each other that have either solid branches or a crotch in the trunks at about the same height. Using trees at different elevations on a hillside or across a ravine can help. Throw one rope over one tree, and the second over the other. Tie off the ends of the ropes to your food bags. Raise the food by pulling on both ropes at the same time, and secure the ends of the ropes by wrapping them

BEAR HANG
(TWO TREE HAULING TECHNIQUE)

around the tree. (One really long rope can replace two ropes in this method as well).

If you have a heavy ration to hang, another option is to create a high line with a single rope between two trees. In this situation, tie a couple of butterfly knots in the rope, clip in a carabiner, attach a haul line to raise your food, and then tighten the high line with a 3:1 pulley. You can have a couple of different attachment points along the high line in this type of set-up. This is the most common system used by NOLS courses where you have 10 to 15 people, each with 10 days of food, which might total 300 pounds. That's like hauling two people into the tree!

High-Line Hang and Tree Climb
Finally, there may be places where you may have to climb trees to set your high line. Make sure the branches on the trees are sturdy; climbers should weight them close to the trunk. Use spotters. Attach one end of the rope to one tree by wrapping it around the trunk and clipping the rope back onto itself. On the second tree, place a piece of webbing around the tree trunk and clip the rope through. Build a 3:1 pulley system on the ground to tighten the line.

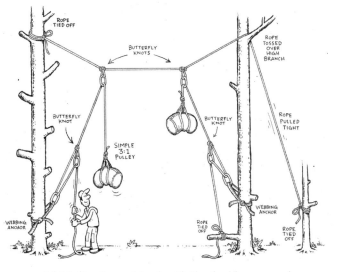

A high line is combined with the double-rope and pulley technique.

Then raise the food as described above. Be careful of falls and falling limbs. If you have enough rope, make all tie-offs at ground level so you can retrieve the system without climbing again. As a warning, NOLS has roughly ten times the injury rate from climbing trees than we have from actual bear injuries.

If the ropes are long enough, it is best to tie them off away from the actual tree where the food will be hung. This reduces the chance of a bear shredding the rope while trying to climb the tree.

Counterbalance Food Hang
In this case you hang a rope over a stout limb with your food bag hanging on one side and a comparably weighted rock or water jug hanging on the other. If you have lots of food, you can also balance two different food bags (one on each side) and forget about trying to tie a rope to a rock. Ideally the stout limb is 20 feet high so you can pull food all the way to the branch, attach your counterbalance, and then push the counterbalance weight up beyond a bear's reach. Note that bears in Yosemite have now learned how to get counterbalanced food. It's like *Spy vs. Spy* out there in the Sierras.

Food Storage in the Arctic Tundra
Bear camping practices are slightly different in Alaska and western Canada from those listed above. In wide open Arctic tundra, the bears are less likely to be habituated to humans, and you usually won't find trees suitable for hanging food. Bears are also hunted by humans in these areas, which may increase their fear of humans. For these reasons, NOLS courses on

open tundra often leave their food bags on the ground in their kitchens at night. You can sometimes hang food over a cliff, toss a line over a large boulder, or find some other creative way to keep your food out of a bear's reach. Note, however, that bear avoidance techniques—such as making noise while hiking, separating tent and kitchen sites by at least 100 yards, traveling in groups of four or more, and carrying bear spray—are the same in this environment.

Electric Fences

NOLS sometimes uses portable electric fences to help deter bears. The school developed these fence systems with the assistance of Wyoming Game and Fish, the Wyoming Animal Damage Management Board, the U.S. Forest Service, the U.S. National Park Service (Alaska Region), the Grizzly and Wolf Discovery Center, many members of the Interagency Grizzly Bear Committee, and advice from many bear scientists. Others have developed fences too, but NOLS invested over $50,000 and spent years gathering data on how fences performed in various field conditions around the world before having custom fences and energizers built to our specs.

NOLS developed and tested this electric bear fence as a reliable means of deterring bears from camp food. Fences such as these are best used in combination with other essential bear country camping practices.

These fences are used for convenience in the backcountry, and, in many places, we get along just fine without them. We still teach students how to hang food and take all other routine precautions. Electric fences don't replace the sound judgment or the normal precautions we should take when we choose to live in bear habitat. Fence users must routinely test each fence setup with a special voltmeter to ensure that it is working properly, and they must be ready to quickly switch to an alternative system if their fence isn't working properly.

These fences use poly wire, which is twisted plastic with a few metal strands woven into it, and we carry the fences rolled up in nylon bags to protect them. The metal strands in these wires are electrified by battery-powered energizers that put out 9,000-volt pulses of electricity once every second. This spark is hot enough to sting, but its amperage is 100 times weaker than would be needed to harm animals (or humans). NOLS' custom-made fence energizer was built based on analyzing electric fence systems on NOLS expeditions. The energizer's backup systems help reduce the human errors common with portable electric fence systems and, as of this writing, have worked for over 50,000 nights in prime bear habitat with no problems.

Although some public campgrounds, like Lake Louise in Banff, have electric fences around entire campgrounds and it works really well for them (Parks Canada, 2008), we do not use electric fences in campgrounds around individual campsites because bears leave their shocking experience quite mad and this may not be good for the people camped just outside of the electric fence. NOLS only uses electric fences in the backcountry, far away from other campers, and oftentimes we only store our food inside the fence, pitching tents outside and well away from the food cache.

A *food storage* fence looks like a 3-foot high volleyball net in a circle 10 feet wide. The NOLS fence is easily set up in a minute or two (a bear hang can easily consume an hour). Extensive testing showed that a pentagon shape endured storms better than other shapes did. Color-coded alternating positive and negative current wires on self-grounding posts reduce some common human errors associated with electric fences. These features especially improved reliability in less than ideal conditions like on course soils, dry conditions, or on cold dry snow. The complete kit weighs six pounds and can store a ton of food. This is an excellent choice for a large group or a long expedition. One drawback is that the fence is a little awkward to pack because of the long stakes.

These fences are available commercially, but the commercial models aren't exactly what NOLS uses, so read and follow each fence system's instructions carefully. For example, most of the features NOLS demonstrated a need for in an energizer are now available on the Sureguard S2 energizer. However, since the S2 is solar powered, it requires special care to keep the panel in the sunlight during the daytime on longer expeditions. There are specific situations when we *don't* use portable electric fences, like if the ground is too frozen for the stakes, or in deep, drifting snow. These fences are also controversial when used without bear-resistant food containers in some areas, so once again be sure to know local agency regulations and land manager bear-camping guidelines, and carefully read the instructions that came with your fence.

A *camp fence* looks like a portable pasture that horse people use with a fiberglass stake every 20 feet (12 m) and a strand of poly wire running from post to post; a single strand at waist height keeps horses in. Bear campers start with a strand at knee height to keep bears out. Bears are diggers, not jumpers. NOLS' testing with captive bears showed that wires were almost never too low to deter bears, but at 3 feet (1 m) high they were too high. The ideal camp fence has two hot wires at 1 foot and 2 feet off the ground, to keep both adult bears and cubs out. For a more permanent camp, or if you have poor soil conditions, put hot wires at 1 and 3 feet, and then put a ground wire at 2 feet. Making the ground wire a more neutral color causes the bear to focus on a highly visible hot wire instead, helping them get the feedback they need if they choose to investigate your fence. Motivated bears *can* get through these fences, but they usually choose not to. Keep a clean camp, just as you would if you didn't have a fence, and the combination of your presence and the camp fence should help you sleep with no worries. When we tested this system at Katmai National Park (see John's tent on the back cover), we saw 40 to 60 bears a day, and the hair on one of our posts showed us that a bear tested our fence the first night, after which no bears attempted to come into our camp.

Another feature of the NOLS bear fences are blinking LED lights so animals can see them on dark nights. We are thoroughly convinced, based on research, that blinking LEDs, or some sort of light warning system, eliminates the problem of bears or other animals accidentally stumbling into the fence. Without lights, we had fences knocked over roughly once in every 1,000 nights. Since adding lights, we have gone over 50,000 nights without a single fence knocked down. Also, animal behaviorists (like psychologists for wildlife) tell us that if a bear clearly sees the fence first, it is more likely to learn from the negative stimulus of the fence shock, as compared to just getting shocked unexpectedly and not seeing the source of the shock.

Electric fences can be very convenient, and can help campers sleep better at night, but they are just one more tool in your bear toolkit. Like with most tools, how carefully you use it will be the primary factor in how well it works.

Fishing & Hunting
IN BEAR COUNTRY

For many folks, fishing and hunting is why we go into the woods. Nearly 45 million Americans fish and hunt every year, and, quite often, they are traveling in bear country. If you are successful—that is, if you are fortunate enough to bring a fish to the net or kill a game bird or animal—suddenly you have food. It's food for you, but it is something bears enjoy as well.

Fishing and hunting in bear country—and how you care for the quarry after you have caught or shot it—is often counterintuitive to how you otherwise live and move in bear country. No elk hunter—or at least no elk hunter who is serious about killing an elk—walks through the woods making a lot of noise or wearing bear bells. And fishermen don't often fish in garrulous packs.

There are a few things you can do to manage risk in bear country whether you are

merely pursuing fish and game, or if you have
harvested a fish or game animal.

FISHING

We have all seen pictures of the fly fisherman
thigh-deep in an Alaskan salmon stream cast-
ing perfectly while a pack of brown bears fish
in the background. You have probably even
heard tales of bears actually stealing fish right
off the line. Fishing, whether on a Michigan
trout stream or an Alaskan salmon river, often
puts the angler on a literal collision course
with bears.

Getting There

When moving through the country, bears often take the easy route. They like well-traveled paths and often move through streamside willow and alder thickets. So do fishermen. When fish spawning runs are in full swing, bears and humans alike flock to the streams and encounters are almost guaranteed.

Much like we teach our hikers, as you approach a fishing spot, especially one with lots of vegetation, it is a good idea to make some noise. If you are traveling with friends, strike up a conversation. If you are alone, you can sing or talk to yourself. Passersby may think you a bit off the rocker, but the idea is to let a bear know you are in the neighborhood. Remember, too, to be on the alert for bear signs. Tracks in the mud, scat, well-worn paths in the willows—all of these are indicators that bears are nearby. Make more noise or go somewhere else.

If you are fishing and you see a bear approaching, give ground. Make noise to let the bear know you are there. If the bear still comes your way, move away. Even if you have the catch of the lifetime on your line, you should ask yourself what is more important:

the fish or your life. If you have hooked into a fish, the Alaska Department of Fish and Game recommends that you try not to let the fish jump. If the bear is close, break off the fish, or cut the line. Retreat and live to fish another day.

In general, grizzly or brown bears are the fishermen of the bear world. But black bears also catch and eat fish. A bear—black, brown, or blue—is an opportunist who is always on the hunt for food. Fish are food.

After the Catch
Even if you are strictly a catch-and-release angler, the smell of fish will get on your hands. If you catch fish to eat, you will get even fishier.

For the catch-and-release angler, getting rid of fish scent is fairly simple. After you have handled your catch, give your hands a quick rinse in the water. Back at camp, scrub up with soap.

Do not wipe your fishy hands on your waders, shirt, hat, or pants. If you use a net, remember that it, too, smells of fish. Give it a rinse and store it away from where you will be sleeping or living in bear country.

If you plan to cook and eat the fish you catch while still in the backcountry, you will want to take even more precautions. In bear country, that means cleaning your fish. You will get fish smell all over your hands when you do this. Rinse your hands well. Dispose of the fish entrails properly. In the backcountry, that often means pitching the guts into the stream or river. Do not leave them on the bank of the stream because they will attract bears. Keep only enough fish to eat that evening, and you will not have fish storage problems.

When cooking fish in bear country, it is a good idea to put the clothes you wear while cooking into the bear hang and then live and sleep in other clothing. Fish smells have a way of penetrating all of your clothes, so keep in mind that you do not want to get into your sleeping bag smelling of fish.

Always wash your dishes and anything that came into contact with the fish, and store all of these things well away from where you are sleeping.

HUNTING

Hunting in bear country is even more problematic than fishing, especially in grizzly bear country. Every year, hunters in North America get chewed on by bears. Why? First, hunting

B iologists have found a direct correlation between grizzly movement in Yellowstone National Park and hunting seasons held outside the park. Just prior to the hunting seasons, the bears will move toward the boundaries of the park. When hunting season starts, they move out of the park and begin feeding on the various gut piles left by successful hunters. Hunters create what biologists call an 'eco-center,' which is essentially a food source much like a salmon stream or a berry patch. Each year around Yellowstone, an estimated 500 tons of bear food are available to bears as the result of successful hunts.

—From *Great Wyoming Bear Stories*
by Tom Reed

calls for stealth, which calls for quiet, which can lead to surprising a bear. Many bear attacks are the result of surprising a bear, and a surprised bear generally thinks that the best defense is a strong offense. Second, if you are a successful hunter, you will have meat to deal with. From field dressing the animal to storing the meat, success means that the bear grocery store is open. Bears live by their stomachs, and are slaves to their noses.

On the Hunt

You move stealthily and steadily. You keep your eyes to the ground for signs of tracks, you listen and smell, and all of your senses are alive. This is the reason many people love hunting, for it is as close to nature as a person can get in this world of personal computers, video games, and automobiles. If you are a good hunter, you will be cautious and quiet as you move through deep woods. Paradoxically, if you are good, you have a tremendous opportunity to run into a bear.

In grizzly country, it is a good idea to hunt in pairs or threes. You will make more noise, but if you are near a hunting companion, you have better odds of avoiding a bear attack if you can bunch up.

Carry bear spray. If you are bow hunting in grizzly habitat, some states prohibit carrying a sidearm, so bear spray is a necessity. Bear spray has been proven over 90 percent effective in repelling charging bears and is more likely to be used accurately under stress than the precision accuracy required for a pistol shot.

Avoid bear encounters by avoiding likely bear hidey-holes. This means avoiding places where bears are likely to be at times when they're likely to be there. In grizzly country, that's thick dark timber during the middle of the day—a place and time where grizzlies like to take midday naps. Hunt away from north slopes at this time of day and you are less likely to put yourself in the path of a bear. Jumping a grizzly out of such a "day bed" is not a pleasant experience.

You can avoid bear encounters by ending your hunt a couple of hours before last shooting light. True enough, this also decreases your chances of seeing game during those crepuscular times—the witching hour when many game animals are on the move. By stopping your hunting in late afternoon rather than early evening, however, you are eliminating the possibility of running into a roaming bear on the prowl; and if you kill game late in the day, you will have a carcass to deal with when it gets dark. The latter is tailor-made for a grizzly encounter. If you kill game late in the day, you might have to abandon the carcass at dark to return the next day. Many, many hunters have made the unpleasant discovery of a bear eating their game when they return the next morning.

After the Kill

Some anecdotal evidence shows that bears in the Greater Yellowstone ecosystem have learned to associate rifle shots with food. On Kodiak Island, wildlife biologist Victor Barnes refers to this as the dinner-bell effect. That means a bear will start moving toward the rifle shot with the hopes of a quick meal. The fact that bears often appear shortly after an animal is harvested is probably as much related to the fact that there are a lot of bears, people, game, and the smell of blood and meat in the same area at the same time.

Even if you are a bow hunter who shoots his game quietly, dead game animals mean blood and meat. Your clothing and hands will smell of blood and meat. You will have a carcass to field dress and you will have meat to retrieve.

When the excitement of the kill wanes, it is a good idea to have a plan for how to deal with the dead animal. The strong scent of a fresh kill attracts bears, and most hunters focus very narrowly on field dressing the carcass, easily creating a surprise encounter. Many experienced hunters believe a can of bear spray is as important as a knife and bone saw at this time. Experienced guides in grizzly country often ask their clients to stand guard with bear spray out and within reach as they gut the fallen game.

Getting the meat away from the kill site is critically important because the kill site is the place where the entrails, blood, and smell of the kill permeates the air. In the unfortunate event that you have to leave some or all of the meat out at the kill site overnight, you can take a couple of precautions. If you can, try to hang the meat up in a tree, even if it is not a classic "bear hang." The idea is to make the meat a little less convenient and hope that a roving bear focuses on the entrails and other humanly inedible portions of the meat. If you can carry the meat away from the kill site before hanging it in a tree, all the better.

Ideally, though, you will have taken the meat away from the kill site back to your camp or vehicle and will not need to return. If you leave a kill site and have to return, flag a trail back through wide open areas, and then go back in making as much noise as possible. The point is to maximize your viewshed, especially as you reapproach the carcass. Try and view the carcass from a distance. Watch for indications that the carcass has been disturbed or fed on. If you are an elk hunter who uses horses to pack out the game, you will make plenty of noise on return, but even so, you should laugh, talk, yell, and make as much noise as possible when coming back to the kill site.

Many times, if a bear has claimed the carcass, it will retreat at the sound of a person coming in. But even if a bear has taken off, if there is evidence of a bear in the neighborhood, such as a cache, scat, or tracks, it is a good idea to either get the meat and get out as soon as possible, or—if your game has been claimed—retreat altogether. You probably will not be able to go kill another elk that season, but sacrificing a game animal to a bear is better than risking your life.

In Camp

The best hunting camps have bear hangs that have been established by federal agencies (like the U.S. Forest Service) or built by private parties. It flies in the face of Leave No Trace ethics to build permanent bear hangs, but practicality has won out and there are many bear hangs being built in heavily hunted bear country. Game meat like elk and deer is very difficult to hang out of bear reach without the use of meat poles.

Hang the meat well away from your sleeping area. Even better, hang the meat well away from any place you are likely to spend a lot of time, like a kitchen area. Some of the best bear hangs are 100 or more meters from camp and downwind of the prevailing breezes. If you store meat in camp, you will have bears in camp. You would rather have them down at the meat hang than in your kitchen; biologists with movement-sensitive cameras have documented many bears sniffing around the meat pole. If the meat is taken care of properly and is out of a bear's reach, the bear will investigate and leave. If it gets a food reward, it will be back.

Everything associated with the kill should be out of bear reach. If you have to skin the carcass or trim blood-shot meat, it is better to do those things well away from camp, preferably at the kill site. Clothing that you wear when dealing with the harvested animal should be hung on the meat pole or otherwise kept away from the bear's reach.

A Hungry Bear

Every year Dave makes a trip into grizzly country in Wyoming's Absaroka Mountains in the national forest outside Yellowstone National Park. Almost every year, someone in his hunting party kills an elk. That means meat to deal with.

In September 2007, Dave killed a nice bull elk that he quartered and hung on a bear pole, far off the ground and far out of bear reach. Or so he thought. During the first night, a bear—probably a black bear—made its way into camp, climbed a tree, and very athletically reached over from the tree to the hanging elk.

Dave read the evidence in tracks and claw marks the next morning. The bear had either leapt from the tree and hung onto the carcass while eating, or had reached over and pulled the carcass to the tree where it could eat. Either way, the better part of a whole elk disappeared into the bear's belly in one evening.

Lands managers recommend that a bear pole be 15 to 20 feet off the ground—thus the bottom of the elk or deer quarter will be at least 10 feet off the ground—and the carcass should hang four feet away from the vertical trunk of the tree. Dave measured the distance of the meat from the tree trunk—three feet, ten inches. Those two inches apparently made the difference.

The best way to deal with bear food in bear country—be it game meat or fish—is to harvest and leave. But if you must stay several days after catching a fish or shooting an elk, think about the smells associated with your quarry and take precautions.

Fishing and hunting in bear country is a rewarding experience. Your senses are heightened and your sense of adventure soars. Bears and quality fishing and hunting often go together. You will have to make common sense decisions, but you will also experience some of the wildest things left on our tamed planet.

Bear
CONFRONTATIONS

Bears are highly complex animals and each bear is a unique individual, so it is impossible to predict exactly how any bear will respond in an encounter. However, studies suggest some actions seem to be more effective than others in responding to specific scenarios. Before we suggest how to react, let's review the top ten bear behaviors so you can think like a bear. This might help you understand all of this.

1. Bears are wary of humans and may react aggressively in self-defense if they think you are going to hurt them or steal their food.
2. Sows invest a lot of energy in raising offspring, so they are extremely protective of their cubs.
3. Bears sometimes attack other bears. Since they primarily bite each other, they try to disarm their opponent by biting its mouth.

And so it is with humans. Research in Alaska shows that bears attack the heads and necks of humans nearly five times more than other parts of the body.

4. Bears have an exceptional sense of smell. They have average hearing, average (color) vision, average night vision, and they especially notice movement during daylight.

5. Most bears can run more than 50 km per hour (30 mph, or two-minute miles) and are predators, so they like to chase things that run from them. They almost always (90 percent of the time) chase fleeing humans, and they usually win that game.

6. Prey tends to turn around and run away. This turning tail excites a bear's predatory instincts.

7. Bears act aggressively toward other bears by moving toward each other, vocalizing or popping their jaws, and staring each other down, but it is usually just a bluff.

8. Bears are less likely to attack larger animals, or large groups of people, because of the risk-to-benefit ratio.

9. Very rarely, a bear acts in a predatory manner towards humans, hunting them down for consumption. (Most black bear attacks

are predatory.) If you run into that oddball predatory bear, you'd better have a deterrent like bear spray or a firearm ready to quick draw.

10. Some bears, like some people, are just different. Avoiding close-range surprise encounters eliminates most problems with all bears.

Here are some typical situations a visitor may experience while traveling in bear country and some recommendations on how to handle them.

Bear more than 100 meters away and unaware of you: Quietly leave the area or let the bear move off on its own. If you absolutely must pass that spot (John dealt with this situation with a rapidly rising tide along a cliff in Alaska), give the bear as much warning of your presence as possible before getting any closer to it, and then carefully watch how it responds to you.

Bear more than 100 meters away and aware of you: First be absolutely certain to let it know you are there—talk loudly and calmly and move upwind so it can smell you. Move out of sight slowly, and then leave the area quickly.

Aware bear less than 100 yards away: Help the bear identify you. Speak in a low, firm voice and wave your arms slowly. Do not move toward the bear. Do not turn your back or kneel down in front of the bear. Turn sideways or back up and walk away slowly.

If you are in a group of four or more, stay together. One person points and says, "I see a bear." The group should then gather together, stand shoulder-to-shoulder, and face the direction the bear spotter is pointing. Get the bear spray ready. Stand your ground and speak to the bear in assured, audible tones. Usually a large group will intimidate a bear and it will leave first; if not, stay in your large group and slowly move away, keeping your eye on the bear.

If the bear walks toward you, back away. Drop a non-food item such as a bandanna, camera, or water bottle to distract it.

Charging bear: Stand your ground. Running may excite the bear's chase response. If you are in a group of four or more, try to convince the bear that you are too big to attack. Stay grouped shoulder-to-shoulder, wave your arms, and continue to talk firmly to the bear. If you are alone or in a small group, attempt to

reduce your presence. Stand facing the bear, be quiet, and try not to move. Some bear managers say to avoid eye contact (others dismiss this as folklore). Remember, most charges are bluffs.

If the bear is within the bear spray's range, use it. Shoot in short blasts and aim for the bear's face. Empty the can if the bear approach persists. Be aware that wind speed and direction can have huge effects on your accuracy.

Attacking bear: If you are actually attacked, your response depends on the situation and the species. If a grizzly bear attacks in a defensive nature, such as when surprised or protecting its young, your best option is always to defend yourself with bear spray. If you aren't carrying bear spray, play dead if the bear actually knocks you down. Rather than curling into a ball, as has been previously advised, lie face down with your legs apart. This position makes it more difficult for the bear to flip you over and attack your face. Place your hands behind your neck and keep your backpack on for protection. Recent studies indicate that you should wait to drop and play dead until the bear actually strikes, or when you think it is just about to make contact. Dropping too soon may turn a bluff charge into a mauling.

In the majority of surprise encounters, victims who play dead are not seriously injured or killed. The bear generally bites and swats the victim a few times and then runs away, all within a few seconds. If this happens, stay absolutely still until you are sure the bear has left the area. Getting up too soon could provoke another attack. If mauling continues despite passivity, you may have to change tactics and fight back.

With black bear attacks, which are almost always predatory, most experts recommend defending yourself aggressively rather than playing dead. Climbing a tree may help, but you have to be faster than the bear, and most black bears (and some grizzlies) easily climb trees.

Nighttime bear in camp: Evening is a particularly dangerous time for a bear encounter. Bears are usually seeking food in this situation. If the bear approaches and attacks, playing dead is not suggested. (The bear may perceive you to be capitulating like prey.) Try to scare the bear away by using bear spray, making lots of noise, or throwing things. The best way to avoid having a bear in camp is to keep a clean camp in the first place.

Bears hunting humans: In rare cases—mostly documented in Alaska and usually with black bears—bears may actually pursue humans as prey. The risk of this scenario is greatest during seasons with poor natural feed. The bear follows its victim for an extended period of time before attacking. (This is your clue.) Under such circumstances, you must fight aggressively if attacked. Punch, hit, and stab at the bear to deter it. Aim for its eyes and nose. As always, bear spray is statistically your best option, but with a predatory attack, a firearm is a good option if you are actually defending your life. This may have huge legal repercussions, so like all decisions to use a firearm, know the laws, know the ethics, develop the expertise that comes from practice, and, above all, use good judgment.

BEAR SPRAY
In hundreds of recorded cases, people defending themselves with bear spray received fewer injuries from bears than did people defending themselves with firearms. Bear spray is just capsicum (ground hot red pepper), and it is propelled by a chemical reaction, much like an air bag deploying. You don't want to go to the surplus store and buy the cheap pepper spray made for use on local purse snatchers: you want genuine bear spray that is labeled "bear deterrent spray."

Take your brand new can of bear spray, go out onto the wide open prairie, set out a target 10 feet away, aim downwind (if you don't, you sure will the second time), pull the trigger guard off, and give it a firm half-second pull on the trigger. This gives you a feel for how far it shoots and, especially, how it is significantly influenced by air currents. If there are high

winds that day, you might also get about 1 percent of the experience that a bear gets as the eddy currents bring some of the capsicum back upwind into your eyes, nose, and throat. Now put the trigger guard back on the bear spray and don't test it any more. Wash the nozzle of the can with soapy water at your next opportunity to get rid of the odor. Avoid getting any of the capsicum on your skin.

You can also buy an inert can of virtual bear spray for training purposes. Or better yet, find someone with an expired can they want to get rid of and really go nuts practicing your bear raid drills, but be careful of where you spray that much capsicum because someone might mind. (John and his daughter shot off 24 expired cans behind their rural home, and luckily the only thing it bothered was their chickens.)

Most bear spray shoots 10 to 15 feet. Despite its range, however, bear spray is not always effective because of the following critical factors:

- wind direction relative to bear direction
- wind velocity
- timing of the spray burst relative to the bear location at that instant
- volume, concentration, and dispersal of spray
- whether the can has a current expiration date and whether it has been properly stored out of the heat.

Bear spray needs to be ready to use (think quick draw). Most bear encounters are unplanned because they don't happen when everyone is singing their "Hey, bear!" songs. They happen when it's late in the evening, you've been hiking all day, and you let your guard down, or when you are walking through the willows without even thinking about it. If you are the only one in your group with bear spray, you need to be at or near the front of the group, not straggling behind.

If a bear gets close enough that you can spray it, spray it. In fact, if a bear is messing with you or your gear, your survival—now and in the future—may depend on you giving that bear some negative feedback via your bear spray. That's what it's for.

The decision to carry bear spray is often a choice dictated by local needs as judged by local wildlife managers. In areas where bear spray is recommended, not carrying it and asking what to do if a bear charges is like asking what to do if you crash your car and have chosen not to wear your seat belt. Should you use your hands to cover your face or to brace yourself? These choices are moot compared to just wearing your seat belt or carrying bear spray. If local wildlife managers recommend it, carry bear spray and know when and how to use it.

Correct Bear Spray Storage
First and foremost, read the label. Most labels say to store between 30 and 120° F (0-50° C). Heat degrades the propellant system and extreme heat can even cause the can to explode. But lesser heat, especially in cycles of heating and cooling, can permanently reduce the bear spray effectiveness. Cycles of freezing and thawing have the same deteriorative effect. The bottom line is to keep your bear

spray stored in a stable environment at home and to protect it from hot sun while transporting it in the field. You also need to keep it out of reach of children and pets.

The Federal Aviation Administration won't let you bring bear spray or other aerosols on commercial airliners. In bush planes, bear spray is carried outside of the passenger compartment or in special aerosol safety containers, because an accidental discharge inside the passenger compartment could be indirectly fatal to everyone if it debilitates the pilot. Accidental discharges, just like with firearms, are rare but do happen.

Incorrect Bear Spray Storage
A Wyoming Game and Fish warden almost destroyed his pickup truck when a can of bear spray, which had been left on the dashboard in the sun, exploded, blowing out the windshield and coating the interior of his vehicle with hot pepper. Another can blew up in the center console of a closed up sedan on a sunny day.

NOLS has had at least one case of a can exploding in a backpack that was sitting all day in the hot sun with the bear spray just underneath the black fabric.

NOLS has also had a can of bear spray explode when a backpack was dropped onto it. Be aware of the location of your bear spray in your pack, and be careful how you set down your pack.

A recently expired can was used as a demonstration for some NOLS semester students as we were entering a location with a recent bear problem, and the spray only went 7 to 8 feet. The manufacturer suggested this was because it had been through repeated freeze/thaw cycles while being carried on numerous NOLS mountaineering courses.

The lesson here is that your bear spray will stay more effective through its life if you follow the written storage directions on the label. One day, you just might care how well your bear spray works.

FIREARMS

If you are hunting, a firearm may be a better deterrent than bear spray simply because you are walking around with it in your hands ready to go, and timing is everything in your encounter with a surprised bear. The problem with firearms is that most bears are so tough that the first few shots might just make the bear really mad before it reaches you. Furthermore, very few marksmen can shoot accurately enough to kill a bear outright. A charging bear can rattle even the calmest sharpshooter. It takes considerable expertise and personal composure to aim a bullet less than half an inch wide as accurately as a cloud of bear spray ten feet wide.

Bullets vs. Bear Spray

Statistically, bear spray is a more effective deterrent, but when a firearm is significantly more convenient, go with it. In a large database of bear-human conflicts in Alaska, firearms were 67 percent effective in deterring bears from attacking, but bear spray was 92 percent effective in deterring bears from attacking (Smith, Herrero, DeBruyn & Wilder, 2008). Another way to look at the same data is that 8 percent of the pepper sprayers were still attacked by the bear, but 33 percent of the gun-shooters were still attacked by the bear.

Leave No Trace
& BEAR CAMPING
ESSENTIALS

Bear camping and Leave No Trace make a good match. The principles of the Leave No Trace outdoor ethics program are quite often right in line with good bear camping practices. Those principles include: plan ahead and prepare, travel and camp on durable surfaces, dispose of waste properly, leave what you find, minimize campfire impacts, respect wildlife, and be considerate of other visitors.

PLAN AHEAD AND PREPARE
In bear country, this means having the right information and the right gear so you can make smart choices. As discussed elsewhere in this book, getting to know the country should start long before you leave your home. Purchase the maps, send the emails, and ask the

questions. Long before you pull out of the driveway, you'll know whether you will be traveling in bear country, and, if so, what kind of bears are likely to be in that backcountry and how the locals effectively deal with them.

If you are going into country where regulations or common sense dictate using a bear hang, plan ahead and locate the gear you'll need. This may mean buying ropes and carabiners, or it may mean purchasing or renting bear-resistant food containers.

TRAVEL AND CAMP ON DURABLE SURFACES

In bear country, it is easiest to camp where there are established bear hangs or storage facilities. In places like Yellowstone National Park, for example, land managers require camping at designated sites. Some Yellowstone frontcountry sites have bear-resistant storage boxes for food and other items that might attract curious bears. These sites may also have bear-resistant trash cans and dumpsters. Yellowstone backcountry sites have poles pre-installed so you just need a rope to use their ready-made bear hangs. Many also have bear storage boxes for food. These are huge conveniences that may save you an hour or two of scouting for a site and building the perfect bear hang.

Quite often these designated camping sites are places that are "hardened" by the use of others before you; thus, they minimize impact to the landscape by concentrating use in these heavily-used areas.

Traveling on well-established trails also makes sense in bear country. Many bears, especially those that are not habituated to humans, avoid areas where humans travel frequently.

DISPOSE OF WASTE PROPERLY

Waste odors attract bears. If you minimize waste and dispose of your waste properly, you minimize your chance of attracting a bear. This means putting all garbage, including food scraps, in dumpsters (where they exist). Where there are no dumpsters, it is critical to gather all food scraps and other garbage into plastic bags and store them with your food.

LEAVE WHAT YOU FIND

This principle is important but not very relevant to hiking and camping with bears. On the ecosystem scale, we humans need to leave bears enough habitat to live in. It takes huge tracts of wild lands to support healthy natural populations of bears.

MINIMIZE CAMPFIRE IMPACTS

Your main concern with campfires in bear country is to not have half-burned food items in the coals. Some bears smell this and come to eat the food (and the coals). If bears are a serious concern, avoid grilling greasy meat and other things that drip animal fat onto the coals. Remember, your concern is that by luring bears to this site, and giving them a food reward, you are conditioning them to human food and habituating them to become more comfortable around humans. This is like leaving a landmine for unsuspecting future campers to stumble upon.

RESPECT WILDLIFE

There are many ways you can influence a bear's behavior. The theme of sloppy campers giving food rewards, thereby training bears to become problem bears and resulting in many of these problem bears being destroyed, runs throughout this book. But wildlife watchers need to be careful too.

When watching wildlife, your actions can influence bears in two notable ways. When you "bump" a bear off of its natural feeding site, you cause it to expend energy and chase it off of a preferred site. This is especially important in the critical seasons of early spring, when food-craving, skinny bears emerge from hibernation, and in late fall when hyperphagic (really hungry) bears are putting on fat for their four-month siesta. Fat is literally a chemical battery, and we have no right to interfere with their need to put on fat in the fall, especially nursing females.

In the spray vs. firearms debate elsewhere in this book, Leave No Trace recommends spraying bears with pepper over shooting them with guns, which is generally safer for you too. A wounded bear is a very dangerous bear that could eventually die from its injuries, while a sprayed bear is in no such danger.

BE CONSIDERATE OF OTHER VISITORS

Remember that bears have an incredible memory and are very intelligent. They'll remember where they got their last meal, and they will travel long distances to get back to that last meal. Bear managers who trap problem bears in one area and move them hundreds of miles over many mountain ranges are rarely surprised when that same bear shows up back where it was trapped in the first place.

When you are camping in bear country, remember that this public land belongs to everyone, and someone is sure to come along behind you. If you leave a mess, you leave not only something that is unpleasant for people, but dangerous as well because it could attract and condition bears.

Other visitors are counting on your responsible behavior in bear country. Their lives, and the lives of some bears, may depend on it. It is an interwoven system of respect and responsibility that, much like karma, could come back to bite you, especially if you return to the site yourself.

About the Authors
and Additional Resources

John Gookin is a current NOLS instructor and the curriculum and research manager for the school. He develops NOLS educational resources, making sure the school's 500+ instructors have access to the latest tools in wilderness education. His many outdoor interests and his local search and rescue team keep him busy.

Tom Reed is a former NOLS instructor who currently lives in the mountains outside Bozeman, Montana, and works on public lands issues for Trout Unlimited. He spends much of his time on horseback and enjoys hunting in the backcountry. He is also the author of *Great Wyoming Bear Stories* and *Give Me Mountains for My Horses* from Riverbend Publishing.

ADDITIONAL RESOURCES FOR HIKING AND CAMPING IN BEAR COUNTRY

NOLS maintains bear information at www.nols.edu/bears
- View our online video by Dragonfly Productions
- Get links to regional bear information
- Print your free bear poster
- See extended play information on *NOLS Bear Essentials*

Alaska Department of Fish & Game. 2008. *Electric Fences as Bear Deterrents.* www.wildlife.alaska.gov/index.cfm?adfg=bears.efences.

Hampton, Bruce, and David Cole. 2003. *NOLS Soft Paths.* Mechanicsburg, PA: Stackpole Books.

Herrero, Stephen. 2002. *Bear Attacks*, revised edition. Guilford, CT: Lyons Press.

Interagency Grizzly Bear Committee. www.IGBConline.org.

Masterson, Linda. 2006. *Living With Bears: A Practical Guide to Bear Country.* Masonville, CO: PixyJack Press.

Parks Canada. 2008. *Lake Louise Campground Electric Fence.* www.pc.gc.ca/docs/v-g/oursgest-bearmanag/.

Reed, Tom. 2003. *Great Wyoming Bear Stories.* Helena, MT: Riverbend Publishing.

Russell, Andy. 2000. *Grizzly Country.* Guilford, CT: Lyons Press.

Schwartz. C. C., S. D. Miller, and M.A. Haroldson. 2003. Grizzly bear. Pages 556-586 in G. A. Feldhamer. B. C. Thompson, and J. A. Chapman, editors. *Wild Mammals of North America: Biology, Management, and Conservation*, 2nd ed. Baltimore, MD: The Johns Hopkins University Press.

Smith, T.; S. Herrero; T. DeBruyn; & J. Wilder. 2008. Efficacy of bear deterrent spray in Alaska. *The Journal of Wildlife Management* 72(3).